Materials, Materials, Materials

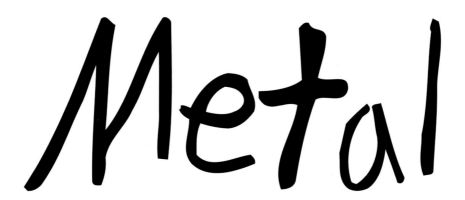

Metal

Chris Oxlade

Heinemann Library
Chicago, Illinois

Designed by Storeybooks
Originated by Ambassador Litho Ltd.
Printed in Hong Kong / China

05 04 03 02 01
10 9 8 7 6 5 4 3 2 1

Library of Congress Cataloging-in-Publication Data

Oxlade, Chris.
  Metal / by Chris Oxlade.
      p. cm. -- (Materials, materials, materials)
Includes bibliographical references and index.
  ISBN 1-58810-155-X
  1. Metals--Juvenile literature. [1. Metals.] I. Title. II. Series.
  TN148 .O9 2001
  669--dc21
                              00-012891

Acknowledgments
The author and publishers are grateful to the following for permission to reproduce copyright material:
Still Pictures/Thomas Raupach, pp. 4, 29; Tudor Photography, pp. 5, 22; Photodisc, pp. 6, 17, 19; Edifice, p. 7; Zul Mukhida, p. 8; PPL Library, p. 11; Still Pictures/Mark Edwards, pp. 12, 13, 26; Corbis/Paul A. Souders, p. 14; Corbis/Yogi Inc., p. 15; Corbis/Peter Johnson, p.16; Stone, p.18; D.I.Y. Photo Library, p. 23; D.I.Y. Photo Library/Photodisc, p. 24; Rolls Royce PLC, p. 25; Still Pictures/David Drain, p. 27.

Cover photograph reproduced with permission of Tudor Photography.

Every effort has been made to contact copyright holders of any material reproduced in this book.
Any omissions will be rectified in subsequent printings if notice is given to the publisher.

Note to the Reader
Some words are shown in bold, **like this.**
You can find out what they mean by looking in the glossary.

Contents

What Is Metal?

A metal is a hard, shiny material found in rocks. There are many different metals. The metal in this picture is aluminum. It has just been made into thin sheets.

Metals are smooth and cold to touch. People make many useful things from metal. Everything in this picture is made of metal.

Hard and Soft

Some metals are very
hard and very strong. It is
difficult to cut or bend them.
The blade of this **saw** is made
of a very hard metal called **steel.**

Some metals, such as lead, are softer and weaker. It is easy to cut or bend them. In some countries, builders bend strips of lead into shape to use on roofs. The lead trim keeps water out.

Electricity and Heat

Most metals let **electricity** flow through them easily. They are good **conductors** of electricity. Here, when electricity flows through the aluminum foil, the light bulb will glow.

Metals also let heat flow through them easily. They are called good conductors of heat. Metal cooking pans let heat flow from the stove top to the food in the pans.

Metals and Magnets

Some metal things stick to **magnets.**
In this game, you use a magnet to pick
up paper fish. This works because each
fish has a metal paper clip on its back.

The only everyday metals that stick to magnets are **iron** and **steel.** The fishing game works because the paper clips are made of steel. So are these cans.

Where We Get Metals

Metals are found in rocks in the ground. The rocks are called **ore.** Workers break up the rocks with tools and **explosives.** Machines dig in the ground and load the pieces of rock into trucks.

People work on the rock to get the metal out. To get **iron** from iron ore, the ore is **melted** in a hot **furnace.** The liquid iron flows out of the bottom of the furnace.

Shaping Metals

Metals can be bent into different shapes. This worker heats **iron** until it glows red. The heat makes the iron soft. Then he shapes it with a hammer.

Metals can also be cut into shapes with tools such as **drills** and **saws.** The tools that do the cutting are made from very hard metals.

Rusting

If **iron** or **steel** things are left in contact with moist air, they turn brown and flaky. They slowly change into a material called **rust.** Some metals, such as gold and silver, never rust.

You can keep things from rusting by painting them. You can also coat them with a metal called zinc. The zinc will keep water away from the iron or steel.

Metals for Electricity

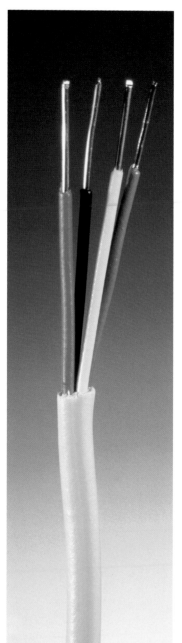

Cables that carry **electricity** around a house have metal wires in them. The metal is called copper.

The copper wires are covered in plastic. This keeps electricity from going from one wire to another wire.

Inside machines such as computers, electricity travels along thin copper tracks on a plastic board. A mixed metal called **solder** is used to stick the copper parts to the plastic.

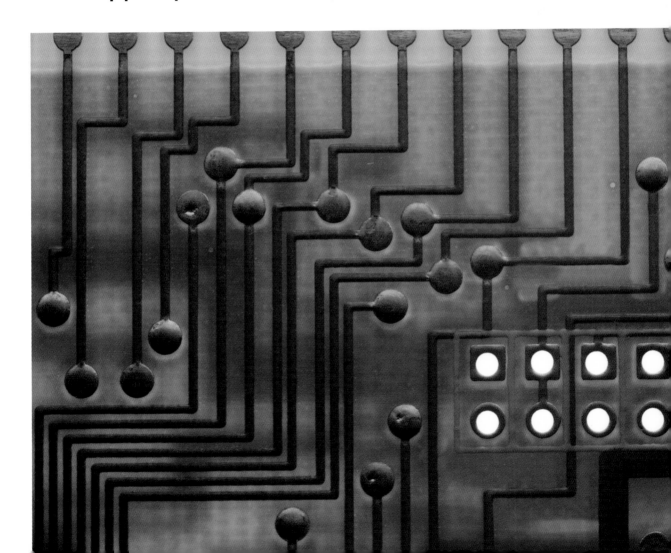

Iron and Steel

Iron is the most common metal we use. It is shaped by **melting** it and pouring it into a **mold,** or cast. This drain cover is made of cast iron.

Steel is made from iron mixed with tiny bits of other materials. It is much stronger than iron. Many tools, cars, and some building **frames** are made from steel.

Aluminum and Copper

The thin foil used to wrap food is made of a metal called aluminum. It is lighter than **iron** or **steel.** Aluminum is also used to make cooking pans and soda cans.

Copper is a reddish-brown metal used to make the wires in **electricity** cables. Some pipes are made from copper, too. It does not **rust,** but it can turn green!

Mixed Metals

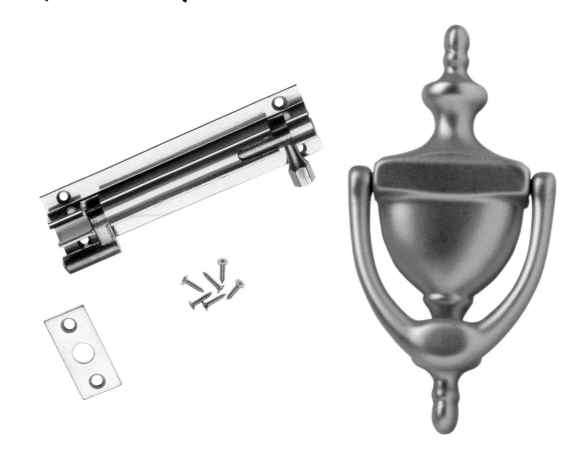

Metals can be made stronger and harder if two or more of them are mixed. Brass is made by mixing copper and zinc. The things on this page are made of brass.

People who build airplanes need metals that are both strong and light. So, plane parts like the one below are made from mixed metals. They are made with metals called aluminum, nickel, and titanium.

Recycling Metals

It takes a lot of **energy** to make metals. This energy is wasted if the metals are thrown away after only one use.

Most metals can be **recycled.** People help by gathering old metal things in special bins. The metal is sorted and **melted** down. Then it is made into new things.

Fact File

▶ Metals are hard, shiny materials.

▶ Metals feel smooth and cold to touch.

▶ Some metals are hard and strong. Some metals are softer and weaker.

▶ All metals allow **electricity** to flow through them. They are good **conductors** of electricity.

▶ All metals allow heat to flow through them. They are good conductors of heat.

▶ **Iron** and **steel** are metals that stick to **magnets.** Most metals do not stick to magnets.

▶ Most metals do not float.

▶ Some metals **rust.**

Can You Believe It?

Gold is a metal that is worth a lot of money. The largest piece of gold ever found weighed more than 200 pounds (75 kilograms). That is as heavy as an adult person!

Glossary

conductor material that lets electricity or heat flow through it

drill tool for making holes in pieces of material

electricity form of power that can light lamps, heat houses, and make things work

energy strength or power to make things move

explosive something that blows up when it is heated

frame part of a building that holds it up

furnace large oven in which materials are melted

iron strong, gray metal that can be heated and formed into different shapes

magnet piece of iron or steel that pulls iron or steel things toward it

30

melt heat a material until it turns from solid to liquid

mold shape into which liquid material is poured in order to form it

ore rock in which metals are found

recycle to use a material again, often to make new things

rust reddish-brown, brittle material that forms on iron or steel when it is left in contact with moist air; or, to turn into rust

saw tool with a sharp, jagged cutting edge called a blade

solder metal made from copper and zinc, often used to join electrical parts together

steel strong metal made mostly from iron

More Books to Read

Bryant-Mole, Karen. *Magnets.* Chicago: Heinemann Library, 1998.

Gibbons, Gail. *Recycle!: A Handbook for Kids.* New York: Little, Brown & Co., 1996.

Madgwick, Wendy. *Super Materials.* Austin, Tex.: Raintree Steck-Vaughn, 1999.

Index